D1717031

Oprah Winfrey
Leader in Media & Philanthropy

by Grace Hansen

Abdo

HISTORY MAKER BIOGRAPHIES

Kids

abdobooks.com

Published by Abdo Kids, a division of ABDO, P.O. Box 398166, Minneapolis, Minnesota 55439.
Copyright © 2020 by Abdo Consulting Group, Inc. International copyrights reserved in all countries.
No part of this book may be reproduced in any form without written permission from the publisher.
Abdo Kids Jumbo™ is a trademark and logo of Abdo Kids.

Printed in the United States of America, North Mankato, Minnesota.

102019

012020

Photo Credits: AP Images, Getty Images, iStock, Seth Poppel/Yearbook Library, Shutterstock,
©Chillin662 p.5/CC BY-SA 4.0, ©ImageCollect.com/Globe-Photos p.7, ©settlja p.11/CC BY-ND 2.0
Shutterstock PREMIER p.cover,19,21

Production Contributors: Teddy Borth, Jennie Forsberg, Grace Hansen
Design Contributors: Dorothy Toth, Pakou Moua

Library of Congress Control Number: 2019941229
Publisher's Cataloging-in-Publication Data

Names: Hansen, Grace, author.

Title: Oprah Winfrey / by Grace Hansen

Other title: Leader in media & philanthropy

Description: Minneapolis, Minnesota : Abdo Kids, 2020 | Series: History maker biographies | Includes
    online resources and index.

Identifiers: ISBN 9781532189005 (lib. bdg.) | ISBN 9781532189494 (ebook) | ISBN 9781098200473
    (Read-to-Me ebook)

Subjects: LCSH: Winfrey, Oprah--Juvenile literature. | Television talk shows--Juvenile literature. |
    Actresses--Biography--Juvenile literature. | Businesswomen--Biography--Juvenile literature. |
    Television personalities--Biography--Juvenile literature. | Oprah Winfrey show (Television program)-
    -Juvenile literature. | African American women entertainers--Biography--Juvenile literature.

Classification: DDC 791.4502 [B]--dc23

Table of Contents

Early Years

Oprah Gail Winfrey was born on January 29, 1954, in Kosciusko, Mississippi. Her childhood was difficult. But through it all, her grandmother supported her.

Mississippi

Welcome To
KOSCIUSKO

LIONS
INTERNATIONAL

ROTARY
INTERNATIONAL

Oprah's grandmother taught her to read aloud by age three. When she was a young teen, she moved to Nashville, Tennessee. Her father, Vernon, lived there.

Nashville, Tennessee

Vernon Winfrey

7

Oprah's father was strict. He made sure she went to school and studied. Oprah did very well on the speech team at her high school. She was also an honors student.

The Beginning of a Big Career

Oprah earned a full scholarship

to Tennessee State University.

A local radio station hired her

part time to read the news.

After graduation, Oprah landed a job with a local Nashville TV station. She was the station's youngest news **anchor**. She was also the first black female to do the job!

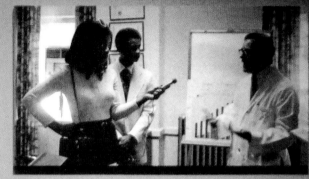

BALTIMORE 1976-83

NASHVILLE 1972-76

CHICAGO: EVERYBE LOVES OPRAH!

BALTIMORE:
PEOPLE ARE TALKING

In 1976, Oprah Winfrey left Nashville to accept a job at WJZ-TV in Baltimore. But she struggled to find her place at the station, where a white male co-anchor made her feel unwelcome, and she felt pressured to modify her appearance. After being demoted from the news desk, she agreed to co-host a new daytime talk show, *People Are Talking*. Although reluctant at first, to walk away from news reporting, Winfrey discovered the talk show format was a better match for her personality and talents.

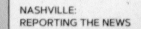

NASHVILLE:
REPORTING THE NEWS

Oprah Winfrey got her first broadcasting job as a 17-year-old high school senior in Nashville when she was hired to read the news on WVOL-AM, a radio station that served the local black community. She transferred to television in 1974 as a reporter for WLAC-TV, which held a unique position: the city's first African-American special anchor, Bill Perkins, and first female feature reporter, Ruth Ann Leach. During her tenure at the station, Winfrey became the first woman to co-anchor the television news in Nashville.

In 1976, Oprah accepted a job in Baltimore, Maryland. She soon began hosting the show *People are Talking*.

Baltimore, Maryland

15

The Oprah Winfrey Show

In 1984, Oprah took a job hosting in Chicago, Illinois. *AM Chicago* was so popular, that in 1985 it was renamed *The Oprah Winfrey Show*. By 1986, it was a national show!

Oprah hosted her talk show for 25 years! Its final episode aired in May 2011.

19

In June 2018, Winfrey and Apple announced a new partnership. Oprah would help create new, original programs for Apple TV+.

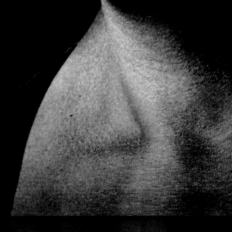

21

Timeline

Oprah moves to Nashville to live with her father.

After college, Oprah moves to Baltimore to begin her hosting career.

Oprah launches *O, The Oprah Magazine*.

Oprah debuts OWN, Oprah Winfrey Network.

1967 **1976** **2000** **2011**

1954 **1970** **1984** **2011** **2018**

January 29
Oprah Gail Winfrey is born in Kosciusko, Mississippi.

Oprah attends East Nashville High school where she **excels** in education and speech team.

Oprah moves to Chicago to host the talk show *AM Chicago*. It is so popular, that it is renamed *The Oprah Winfrey Show*.

May 25
After 25 seasons, the last episode of *The Oprah Winfrey Show* airs.

Oprah announces a partnership with Apple TV+

Glossary

anchor – to serve as a broadcaster by introducing reports and reading the news.

excel – to do or perform better than others.

honors student – a student whose coursework has earned them a place on a school's honor roll.

scholarship – money given to students to help pay for the cost of school.

strict – stern and demanding.

Index

Abdo Kids
ONLINE
FREE! ONLINE MULTIMEDIA RESOURCES

Visit **abdokids.com** to access crafts, games, videos, and more!

Use Abdo Kids code
HOK9005
or scan this QR code!